to: Mom   from: Dave

on the occasion of: Birthday

3/21/1978

May the blessing of light be with you—
    light outside and light within.
May sunlight shine upon you and warm your heart
     'til it glows like a great peat fire
     so that the stranger may come and warm himself by it.
May a blessed light shine out of your two eyes
     like a candle set in two windows of a house,
     bidding the wanderer to come in out of the storm.
May you ever give a kindly greeting to those whom you pass
     as you go along the roads.
May the blessing of rain—the sweet, soft rain—fall upon you
     so that little flowers may spring up to shed their sweetness in the air.
May the blessings of the earth—the good, rich earth—be with you.
May the earth be soft under you when you rest upon it,
     tired at the end of the day.
May earth rest easy over you when at the last you lie under it.
May earth rest so lightly over you that your spirit
     may be out from under it quickly,
     and up, and off,
     and on its way to God.

AN IRISH BLESSING

a photographic interpretation by Cyril A. Reilly and Renée Travis Reilly

Winston Press

Winston Press, Inc.
430 Oak Grove
Minneapolis, MN 55403

The text of this book is set in Caslon Old Face
and printed on 100lb. Northwest Velvet by
Kolorpress, Inc., Minneapolis.

May the blessing of light be with you—

light outside...

and light within.

May sunlight shine upon you...

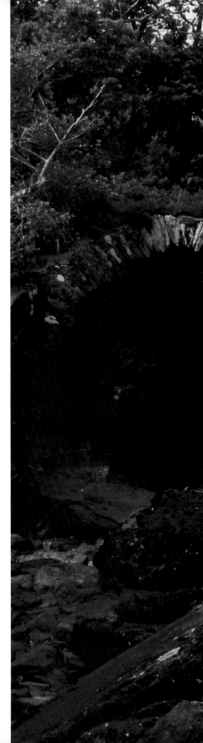

and warm your heart...

'til it glows like a great peat fire...

so that the stranger may come
and warm himself by it.

May a blessed light shine out of your two eyes...

like a candle set in two windows
of a house,

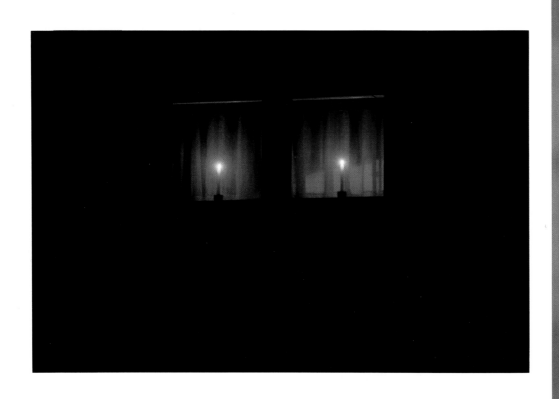

bidding the wanderer to come in out of the storm.

May you ever give a kindly greeting
to those whom you pass...

as you go along the roads.

May the blessing of rain—

the sweet, soft rain—

fall upon you...

so that little flowers may spring up
to shed their sweetness
in the air.

May the blessings of the earth—

the good, rich earth—
be with you.

May the earth be soft under you
when you rest upon it,

tired at the end of the day.

May earth rest easy over you...

when at the last you lie under it.

May earth rest so lightly over you...

that your spirit may be out
from under it quickly,

and up, and off, and on its way to God.

Locations of Special Interest